*the*
# Chasm

Rebecca Anne Perry

the Chasm

Copyright © 2021 Rebecca Anne Perry

All rights reserved. No part of this publication may be reproduced, stored in a retrieval system or transmitted in any form or by any means – for example electronic, photocopy, recording – without prior written permission of the author. The only exception is brief quotations in printed reviews.

For permission, contact Perry 2 Publishing at:
perry2publishing@gmail.com

ISBN: 978-0-578-91714-6

# DEDICATION

This book is dedicated to my Granny.

Her faith grew, persevered, matured and flourished throughout her life. She loved God through the black plague at the turn of the 20th Century, the Great Depression of the 1930s, being in a poor German farming family eking out an existence during the famine of the dust bowl, learning English the hard way in an English-speaking school while the other kids made fun of her German and her poverty, helping to raise her nine younger brothers and sisters (two of whom passed away within months of being born), helping with the farming when she was in her early teens (and quitting school to do so because, for the family, farming was about staying alive), surviving a painfully unspeakable betrayal and abandonment early in her young adulthood, later marrying a man whose salvation she prayed for daily, losing her father too soon, caring for her ailing mother until she passed and then for her dying husband until he passed.

Her unwavering faith, her steadfast life and her unshakable perseverance profoundly inspire me. Her beautiful legacy invites me to greater heights and reminds me that there is *more than just this life*.

This book is dedicated in her honor – in remembrance of the remarkable heart & spirit of an indomitable woman of faith.

# ACKNOWLEDGEMENTS

*John 3:16*

# CONTENTS

| Chapter | Description | Page No. |
|---|---|---|
| | Introduction | 7 |
| 1 | A Branch Broke Off | 9 |
| 2 | Venom Eyes | 20 |
| 3 | Schisms | 37 |
| 4 | Silent Screams | 83 |
| 5 | Laments | 95 |
| 6 | Balm | 106 |
| 7 | Breaking Ground | 125 |
| 8 | Equitable Restitution | 136 |
| 9 | Fanning the Flame | 148 |
| 10 | Herbs | 168 |
| | Epilogue | 208 |
| | About the Author | 210 |
| | Other books by the Author | 211 |

# INTRODUCTION

The layout of this book is ten chapters which follows the format of many of the Psalms in the Bible – that format beginning with crying out to God, processing through feelings and circumstances, and reaching a conclusion of trusting in God to do what only He can do. As with many of the Psalms, this process in life is not a one-time event. It is repeated as often as needed. It is essential to show oneself grace along the way as one processes the countless challenges and trials that are part of this life and this broken world.

In this book, I share my processing of the wounds I have suffered from others, many of them from other women – sisters, co-workers, friends, allies, leaders, acquaintances and passers-by. In spite of these wounds, I continue to seek and nurture healthy relationships with women that empower us each to become more fully ourselves, more confident in our gifts, calling and boldness in Christ.

The wounds from men are just as devastating, though harder for me to express because of what I believe God intended men to be – protectors. To voice the betrayal of a protector is difficult and often horrific. To my brothers in Christ, I invite you to consider the damage you create when you fail to protect and defend against evil, or worse, when you yourself are the instrument of harm. Return to Him and to what He created you to be. It is never too late for redemption's work to begin.

Some wounds, too, are from myself. Those are harder to acknowledge and address. But I have found that acceptance is a good place to begin to heal from within. Dealing with these self-inflicted wounds is actually some of the greatest breakthroughs that I have experienced. The battle within brings the most rewarding freedom.

This book also touches on some of the divisions that I see in our world and culture that hold us back from being more fully human and more fully connected to one another. I ache to see unity in the body of Christ in the way that Jesus prayed for us all to be united – in love.

This book is an invitation to people to wrestle with God, to pour out their hearts to Him and see how He responds. It is a challenge to enter into a process of surrendering to God and accepting themselves and others, just as they are.

I wrote this book to remind myself of what's inside of me and each person on earth. The heart of this work of art is that of a person who is fierce, fiery and unbreakable. We have no idea, yet, what lies in wait for us in the future. Our purpose, our calling is not yet completely fulfilled.

This poetry is to remind myself and other people how powerful and fruitful the process is that takes place inside of each person. It is intended to refresh others in knowing that the quiet waiting seasons are pregnant with blessings that they did not even dare to think of or imagine asking for. People are more than they know or realize. I see more in the people I meet than they often do. I am expectantly excited about the great things I believe will happen for, through and in each person.

I have not yet attained all that I seek – all of the wisdom, healing, restoration and recompense. But I continue to pursue these things and the changes in me that will make room for them. I am a work in progress, a broken mess becoming glorious in the process of being "under construction." I pray my journey encourages you on your own pursuit of adventure, answers and acceptance.

# 1 – A BRANCH BROKEN OFF

## *Chapter One – Introduction*

A branch broken off is the poetry of, from and in rejection. This is the poetry of the pain and sorrow of these harrowing experiences. It is known only in the vacantness of an outcast, the vagrance that anguish can outlast. It is the agony of being alone within and without.

This poetry is the outcry of a lone nomad who knows an infinite sadness and is in search of a place to belong, a people to call home. It is a test and a trial that imparts an ability to rest even in the fire. The soul's desire is to live such a life that is above the mire of the strife in this life.

## Another Rejection

Am I not *worthy*
      of connection?

Are you *that* afraid
      of rejection?

You'd rather be *alone*
      than take a risk on?

You'd *prefer* to stay the same
      than make a change?

You choose to be aloof
Let it be your noose
Your life is proof
You'd rather die than lose

## Codependent Rejection

Codependency
Is coercive dependency
It is one person
Coercing another
To depend on
Him or her

It is an utter rejection
Of free will and freedom

It fears rejection
So it violates freedom
                to manipulate
                to exert control
                to dominate
                              a person's soul

## Defending Her In Nonsense

I ache of
The emptiness
In being
   Forgotten

I am emptied
And waiting
For something
   To fill me

She un-named me
In her maniac deceit
To silence me
   From truth speaking

She un-made me
To specificity
That only she
   Could spew easily

Her words vomit up
Lurking, stewing hatred
The bitter bile of
   Craven vengeance

The stench of her breath
Belies an evil bent
She gives herself over
   To who holds her prisoner

She stays in this pain
To deny the stain
On her sullied name
   She chooses to remain

In the sand goes her head
To avoid what she dreads
Confronting the truth
                      The trauma of her youth

**Enough**

It's just
        not enough

Their paltry crumbs
scattered on the ground
for me to scrounge

It's just
        not
                what I want

What I need
is family

They won't
offer
that to me

They withhold everything
I need
yet act like it's nothing

I can't be in close proximity
to people who ignore me
but call it loving

                                          It's not enough
                                            for me

## Failing and Standing (not failing to stand)

So this is failure?
Powerless to stop it
I didn't cause it
Yet, in failure – I stand

The fire of failure
                        doesn't burn
As much as I thought
                        it wood

                                      Whether
                                      In the fire
                                    Or the choir
                              In the seeming defeat
                                Or honest victory
                                          I stand

## No One – Not One

I was sad
        and no one saw

I was mad
        and no one heard

I was hurt
        and no one cared

I was scared
        and no one helped

I was…
        …and now I'm not

                because Someone
                sought me
                saw me
                sobbed with me
                sung to me
                stayed by me

## Scene Unseen

She was scene
I was not

It's as simple
As all that

I wanted to be seen
I wanted my voice heard

Somehow – hers was
To be scene and herd

I pondered this
Insignificance

It seemed only
To assault me

Invisibility
Is not so super

Nothing to it
To marvel

Though…the trolls
Don't seethe me

I guess that's something
Good in being un-scene

## Silent or Quiet

Are you silent
Because you believe
Your voice doesn't matter to me?

OR

Are you quiet
Because you perceive
My heart doesn't matter to you?

# 2 – VENOM EYES

## *Chapter Two – Introduction*

The poems in this chapter concern betrayal of many sorts. Betrayal is a poison that is willfully injected into a relationship by one person with or without the knowledge or consent of the poisoned one. Betrayal burns and stings because it is the toxicity of deception and the painful realization of disguised rejection (a.k.a. passive aggression).

Betrayal is revenge for a real or perceived wrong. It is a punishment with murderous intent. It is a violation of trust and covenant.

Betrayal – like all other forms of bitterness and resentment – is doubt that God's justice is sufficient. Betrayal is essentially unbelief and faithlessness. If one has faith in God, then one must come to terms with this act of rebellion.

## A Rose In Vain

A rose black
By any other feign
Is a poison rack
Of the same bitter vein

# A Usurper's Throne

She once was "close"
Then turned a ghost
Vapor and mist
Her words she hissed
If her heart breathes
She might yet leave
I don't know what
Will end her glut
She hides her fears
In smiling sneers
The queen's new robes
Not at all clothes
Phony attire
For a liar
Cannot convince
Her subjects wince
See her folly
Insults volley
Until she flees
Reality
To scab again
Denying then
All seen and true
Subdue anew
Confined subjects
Whom she rejects
Worship is all
She takes from all
Nothing suffices
Her like her vises

## Blackened Pain and Rage

Battles rage
Because it's an easy way
To avoid pain

Anger and hate
Serve to evade
Torment and ache
Internal pervade

## Black Rose

The blackest rose
Is the one
That grows
In her home

She is a bitter
Pretty little biter

Her sugary bile
Stings as it clings
And claws at my
Heart once trusting

A sister is a murderer
A thieving marauder
Vile in her cunning
Rage coats her lying
With poison meant to kill
My voice and life to be still
Merciless bent of hatred
Drives her mad mind red
She has to destroy me
To hide her villainy
To bury the truth…

She hates the truth

## Choosing Cycles Vicious

She chose
Deceit

Herself
She chose

It's what
She wants

She can change
                Her mind later
                                If she wants

## Cultivating Confusion

She uses
The people that
She confuses

She denies
The actions that
She contrives

She hates
The life that
She cultivates

## Dogs and Dregs

No one
Would torture dogs
If their own
Inner agony was resolved

No one
Would drown in dregs
If their own
Torment lost its legs

No one
Would mistreat dogs or dregs
If their own
Community cared to accept
The need to heal
The internal suffering

**Flesh Fed**

She
Has figuratively
Ripped off my flesh
To feed herself

She
Has gorge-ously
Shredded my character
To greed her further

She
Has famished-ly
Defamed my given name
To fiend her game

## Python is a Brother

Broad knowing grin
Head tilt down shaken
S-l-o-w drawl
Bitter gall
Overbearing stall
Condescending voll

This python
Appalling un-dawned
Oppressive weight
Of writhing hate
Slunk and gone
Beneath, beyond

He lies in wait
Years, decades
Months, days
Bile in his bait
To eliminate
His fear in hate

To trust this one
Is not wisdom
The good in him
Is imprisoned
Dark deep within
Stained by untold sin

He fears to begin
To get free again
Something inside him
Hates him
More than
He hates anyone

To fear him
Seems reason
But nothing
It's doubting Him

## Sister Schisms

She is my sister
        and she is not

She is a stranger to me
        yet I see her clearly

She is an apparition
        from which I partition

She stalks me fraught
        and I fear her not

She eschews truth
        when I pursue it with You

She cries – She rages
She condemns
She condescends
        I am confused by
        her incongruity
        but not taken in

She rejects me
        I accept this

She demands I die
so she can lie
that she loves me
        I reject her request
        and say Goodbye

We are threw
                We are through
                              We are thru

## The Ties That Revile

She is a leviathan
Slithering here and anon
Hissing from hidden places
Spitting venom in traces
Evading her exposure
She feigns holy composure
But her eyes speak of darkness
Stingy, wounded viciousness

Their lack of light
Her soul cold night
Is revealed in love's fire
In which can hide no liar

There she is naked, ashamed
Her truth known; her lies named
No more harm can she yet spew
All her rebellion burned through
Whatever is that remains
Will be given a new name

## Un-soul Connections

In blood
but not soul

Not blood
of His own

Her heart
is of stone

A heart
without soul

## Un-soul Connections, Too

She and I are sisters in every way
Except all the ways that matter

We tred no common ground
Our lives are now unbound
Our hearts and minds
Never aligned
To wander apart
Far from the other's heart

It's not love that rages
Against the changes

No, that's fear's voice
That denies choice

Fear seeks to control
The "loved" one's soul
Fear smothers freedom
To raze *the* Kingdom

## Water and Blood

Blood is NOT
                thicker than water

It is more
           deceptive

Not only
           less than water
           less than life
           less than true

It is merely
            watery crimson goo

Blood is
           only blood
Nothing
           more or good

The ties
           of true life
connect
           with the soul

Spirits
           only unite
within
           truth of Light

# 3 – SCHISMS

## Chapter Three – Introduction

Schisms are the differences that people permit and even choose to use in order to create division and enmity.

Schisms are the mechanisms that people utilize to hide behind, to deflect other people from seeing their pain at feeling different and rejected.

Schisms are a giant flashing neon sign to anyone with a modicum of emotional intelligence. These signs shout and scream of the schism-maker's insecurity.

Schisms are scathingly murderous slashes at another person's soul identity and dignity. They sear the mind and mutilate humanity. Often times, the damage is unspeakable. Sometimes, all that can be said is one paragraph, one sentence, one word – and yet this *one* speaks volumes.

For the schism-makers, those hurting haters who hate the others who are hurting…

…this one's for you…

## Divisions

Division
Is the schism
That keeps us impotent

Understanding
Is the thing
That gives us movement

Discussion
Not concussion
Lets the truth rend

Education
Is the station
That lets us exponent

Confession
Not suppression
Lets the wounds mend

Conversation
Is the invitation
That moves us imminent

Diversity
Is the remedy
That keeps us relevant

...with that said
 let's converse...

## Age Schisms – Division Over Age Groups:

### Pounding Changes

Pound sign
Changing times
Generations find
Uncommon's fine

Number sign
Is in line
With a mind
Left behind

Age ain't the sign
That I'm right
Age is the light
That can align

The crux isn't age
It's life's change

Every generation
Gets to forty and complains
The next generation
Is going down the drain

Those in the twenties
Believe there's plenty
They'll make a difference
With their influence

For each age group
I could speak such truth
Reveal to you
Nothing's new

There's a rhythm in and within
All of the generations

A push and a pull
An ebb and a flow
If you're not so dull
Open your eyes to know

*Generational Monikers:*
The Lost Generation
The Greatest Generation (a.k.a. the G.I. Generation)
The Silent Generation (a.k.a. the Lucky Few)
The Baby Boomers (a.k.a. the Me Generation)
Gen X (a.k.a. the Latchkey & MTV Generation)
Millennials (a.k.a. Gen Y)
Gen Z (a.k.a. Zoomers)
Gen Alpha

*Pondering Generational Patterns:*
High maintenance and high innovation
Low maintenance and low innovation
Stretch and relax
Expand and contract
Tear down and build up

                                Can a generation do both?

Humanity won't end
With your generation

Share your wisdom
In lieu of condescension

                                For the over sixty crowd
                                Who like to be extra loud
                                    Being old is no excuse
                                For being mean and rude

If you're not too proud
To lay yourself down
Impart dignity and wisdom
To the next generation

You are an elder who
Can teach our youth
To do what you do
And something new, too

We need you to get on board
With stepping forward
Into the next big thing
Our generations can bring
When we combine our strengths
To overcome blocks and chinks
Our unity
Is exponentially
Far greater
Then we are

Together we are
The hope coming forth
Illuminating more
Than all that came before

**Youth Truth**

Youth
Is no excuse
To be rude

Truth
Is you need to
Let us teach you

Youth
Is our hope to
Bring us through

Truth
Is we need you
To be you

Youth
Is a gift to
See life new

Truth
Is there's no excuse
To not be you

                                                                      What you do
                                Brings something new
                   United is something we must do

                                                We need you
                                    You need us, too
                 *Together* is the best thing we can do

# Body Weight Schisms:

## Sizing Up Worth

Size four
Open doors
Friendly faces smile
Nods of approval
Appreciating glances
Invited to dances

Size twelve
Put it back on the shelf
Unseen and ignored
Unmoved doors
Sneering faces
Disapproving grimaces

Sizes
Define us
As acceptable
To those folks
Who value
Appearance as
A measure of
A person's worth

> To some others though
> Who perceive the soul
> Body mass and weight
> Are not character traits
>
> The heart of a human
> Weighs more heartily
> On a measuring line
> Of folks who seek to know
> A person's soul

And define worth
By breath in lungs

Sizing up a life
Sizing down the strife
Seizing a moment to be
Seizing the air to breathe

The size of a life
Might be the light
Emanating from eyes
That perceive life
In a generous light
Of loving eyes

# Clothing / Fashion / Style Schisms:

### Whim Worthy

If clothing determined worth
Then worth is *less than* skin deep
Then the value of a person
Is only a thin fabric
That wears out over time
Subject to seasons
Overthrown by a whim

Is a whim worth
Determining a person's worth?

## Quite a Character

A gown or tuxedo
Overalls and cotton clothes
Neither informs nor truly hides
A character that inhabits the mind
Surfaces too often lie
What's inside

## Living Style

Clothes don't know
What's inside my soul

Department stores
Care *less* not more
About my integrity
Than whether I'm credit worthy

Wardrobe choice is not indicative
Of the value and worth of the life I live

My character clothes me
More accurately
Than designer jeans

Do you have eyes to see
The real me?

# Cultural Schisms:

## All the Different

Different hair
Different dress
Different flair
Different mess
All beautiful
All unique
All wonderful
All let us seek
Wonders anew
In me and you

Different food
Different clothes
Different good
Different souls
All opens hearts to know
All invites us to grow
All can share
Some of theirs
To make something
Fresh and exciting

# Faith Schisms:

## Freedom to Believe

I choose to leave
What someone believes
To what they perceive
Faith can be

I believe
Choice is imperative
For faith to be
An honest narrative

If I tried to control
Whether faith you hold
Then I would be an enemy
Of the faith I proclaim to believe

## Loving Humanity

For a Christian
Refusing to see a person
As a godly creation
Is not an expression
Of love for the One

To demonstrate love for God
We must love what He loves
Evidently, He loves sinners
*Like you and me* – like all of us

If His heart matters to us
It must be evident
In how we treat the least of us
Regardless of their bent
Or ours in the moment
We must sacrifice that in us
Which is turned away from Him
So that He can closer draw us

**Vision Beyond Division**

Dissecting denominations
Dividing faith within itself
Creates barriers not conversations
Keeping people from the wealth of nations
Which is the people themselves

Seeking to understand reservations
Can build roads to innovation
Living in harmony and health
Can produce an internal wealth
That abounds in sustaining relations

# Familial Schisms:

## Ditching Dysfunction

Dysfunction
Though common
Is not the end

>                     Hope
>         Does not abound
>         In throwing down

Acknowledging
Dysfunction is a common
Move to begin

>                   Wisdom
>              Is not sound
>       In words without actions

Pursuing
Transformation unto function
Is a lifelong journey

>               Excellence
>             Is not found
>            In stagnation

## Nepotism

Nepotism
Is despotism

Selfishness
And nothing less

Parents who exploit a child
To force on them a life
For which they are unskilled
And is, for the child, unfulfilled
Is a tragedy

How many overtly qualified
Have the parents denied
To transition their business
So they could leave it to less
– Good sense?

How many descendants
Coast on the flippant
Blindness of an ancestor
Who chose to ignore
Good sense?

Children
        listen
It's time to do
              what you can
To produce fruit
              evident
Of what's inside you
                not in them

You are a new thing
A unique being

                              Can you stand
                                  or are you
                                              irrelevant?

## Sibling Incivility

Brothers and sisters
How can we be at odds
When we both love God

I know to you
These odds are much ado
Help me to see
What they mean

I want to speak
To let go and release
Things that have laid desolate
I know it's not too late
If you will give us a chance
To each express our grievance
And move toward
Being restored

I won't force you
So I wait
For you
To feel safe

I'm waiting
For you to bring
What you can
We can begin again

# Gender Schisms:

## Man-*ish* Arguments

Genital-men! Genital-men!
Now that I have your attention
Let us discuss
Your thought process

It seems some of you believe
Genitals control thinking
Unfortunately, scientists
Even some with penises
Have discovered the organ
Contained in the skull
Controls thought and emotion

Your claims against this are null

Now, should you feel a bit irate
Or even begin to spew some hate
I sigh to remind you of
Anger being *gasp* an emotion
Which means if you are mad or see red
You might as well say your vagina bled

You're being emotional
Which as you know is irrational
Of course, it's illogical, too!
Here, would you like a tissue?

If you think you need to suppress me
To secure your so-called supremacy
Then you've already proven your inferiority
With your power play phony superiority

Domination and condescension
Belies your insecure apprehension
That all your blustering aggression
Is just a mask to hide your true expression

The only plan
That proves you're a man
Is
I Am that I Am

Your identity can't be found
In crushing down and pushing around
The only thing you gain
When you annihilate
Is more putrid self-hate
Sinking further into hell's pain

                                        To be a man
                                  Is to face your fear
                                And move through it

A man conquers the beast within
And brings it into submission
To prove his courage
To forge his character
To gain self-respect
Can't be done circumspect
Must confront the specter
Weakness and failings barrage
To gain the ultimate admission
Of respect from the only one
Who matters above all else
That is — himself

Self-acceptance
                *is*
                        Self-respect

I hope you heard me
Loud and clear
All you gentlemen
Far and near

                May God give you strength
                To face each day at length
                With respect and honor in
                Every word and action

## Woman-*ly* Aggression

Ladies! Ladies!
Passively betraying
Is beneath your dignity
It is womanhood massacring

Gender-cide
Seems to be
The theme
Of your life

Cutting off other women
Doesn't bring you the freedom
That you foolishly seek
In the havoc you wreak
On those you perceive
As your enemies

Other women
Aren't your competition

Other women
Won't limit your provision

Other women
Can't thwart your connection

I sigh, I grieve
I want to believe
That together we
Can bring healing
Breathe meaning
Back into femininity
Create a new unity
Birthed in celebrating
What we each bring

To our collective
So we can be more effective
At leading and teaching
In raising and praising
Creating and sustaining
Imparting and regarding

Bonded in honoring worth
Then, we are a valiant force

## Nurturing Mankind

God created a garden
Then a man
God put the man
In the garden
To nurture, to tend
The plants within

God created a woman
To co-labor with the man
In tending the garden

The man and woman
Broke covenant
And fell from grace
To a shame-filled place

Thus, man was nurturing
From the beginning
 – in the garden alone
 – in the garden with the woman
 – before the Fall
 – after the Fall

God created nurturing
In man
But for the Fall
Man would not be afraid
That he is nurturing
Nor try to hide, nor deny
What he now perceives
As a great weakness
His vulnerability
In his nurturing ability

To nurture
Is to flourish
To cause to grow and to gain
To succor and sustain

Whether love or hate
You nurture when you meditate
Whatever your thoughts pursue
Is what's important to you

This is how you nurture
 – by thought, by word, by deed
The path you walk and breathe
Can be lovely or torture

Man can deny
He is nurturing
But only by a lie
He's nurturing

# Intellectual Schisms:

## Intellectually Leveling

Level of intellect
Is not a defect
Nor can it circumspect
A character of ill effect

**Traversing Lines**

Being cultured
Traveling the world
Neither makes one a pearl
Nor a vulture

## Locally Speaking

Staying local
Simple living
Ain't no yokel
Crown no king

# Living Location Schisms:

## Tracks

Tracking value
By a place skewed
Under a lens untrue
To intrinsic view

Tracking identity
On the right side
Of an indiscriminate line
Creates entropy

Tracking along
Defining wrong
Limiting belong
Weathered long

Location of tracks
Gives value to tracts
Denies truth to facts
Separates through fracts
Derails for lacks
Unearned brass tacks
Crushing attacks
Smothered by sacks

Tracks don't define a life
Tracks won't restrain a life
Tracks can't deny a life

# Race Schisms:

## Skin

Skin is only an organ
It does *not* determine
The worth of a person

Skin is an expression
God's poetic imagination
His divine creation

Skin is a covering
of loveliness resting
over a soul fascinating

## Eyes and Trials

Color is perceived by the eye
Character is perceived when tried

The fire of testing trials
Reveals what's inside us

Coloring our lives
Character provides
A sight of life within
To a life enlightened

## Dust Delight

Value is breathed into dust
Breath of the One
Who is in Heaven

Created in His image
For His delight
Apple of His eye

We are all made from dust
Every single one of us
Alive only by His love

## Underdeveloped Intellect

An immature mind
Is one that remains blind
To what exists behind
The covering of hide

Such a mind rages to define
A rule that will bind
The world to an unholy line
Bent to brutally malign

It contorts itself to resign
All of life to a design
That is maniacally unkind
To everyone alive

It loves no one in life
Not even its own life
Hate and fear its only drive
To destroy every life

The solution is found
In teaching what is sound
Turning a heart from stone
Into a life that is known

## Different

Different
Is not deficient
Nor incompetent

Different
Is evidence
That God is infinite

Different
                Is wonderful
                                  Brilliant and magnificent

## Un-Wisdom

Racism
Is an abomination

It's a desecration of
Wisdom

## Fire and Flame – A Laughing Bane

The remedy
Is not more enmity

Fighting flame with flame
(a.k.a. fighting hate with hate)
Is a self-defeating game
(a.k.a. another way to self-annihilate)

The fire of truth and love
Is what heals us

The fear of love and truth
Our wounds that ooze

The antidote
Is faith love hope

Mercy and forgiveness
                      Set us free
                      And burn the enemy
                      Until he sees
                      That his way is futility

Fighting fire with water
Fury with laughter
Defangs and declaws
Those unholy outlaws
They are not so potent
When treated as impotent

Try levity
As an optional remedy

Try eternity
As the hope & future of unending peace

## The Race Against Hate (To Put It To Rest)

RACE RACE RACE RACE RACE RACE RACE R  **Hate**
ACE RACE RACE RACE RACE RACE RA  **Erase**  CE R
CE RACE RACE RACE RACE RAC  **Negate**   RACE RA
E RACE RACE RACE RA  **Subjugate**  ACE RACE RAC
RACE RACE RAC  **Shame**   RACE RACE RACE RACE
ACE RA  **Inhumane**  ACE RACE RACE RACE RACE R
**Degrade**  E RACE RACE RACE RACE RACE RACE RA
**Mutilate**   RACE RACE RACE RACE RACE RACE RAC
RACE  **Defeminate**   RACE RACE RACE RACE RACE
ACE RACE RACE R  **Emasculate**  RACE RACE RACE R
CE RACE RACE RACE RACE R  **Incarcerate**   ACE RA
E RACE RACE RACE RACE RACE RACE R  **Annihilate**
RACE RACE RACE RACE RACE RACE RAC  **Insinuate**
ACE RACE RACE RACE RACE  **Invertebrate**  RACE R
CE RACE RACE RACE  **Invade**  ACE RACE RACE RA
E RACE RACE  **Violate**  ACE RACE RACE RACE RAC
RACE RA  **Bait**  ACE RACE RACE RACE RACE RACE
ACE  **Cage**   RACE RACE RACE RACE RACE RACE R
**Rage**  ACE RACE RACE RACE RACE RACE RACE RA
**Pain**  ACE RACE RACE RACE RACE RACE RACE RAC
RAC  **Blame**  E RACE RACE RACE RACE RACE RACE
ACE RACE  **Devein**   CE RACE RACE RACE RACE R
CE RACE RACE RAC  **Drain**  E RACE RACE RACE RA
E RACE RACE RACE RACE  **Defang**  ACE RACE RAC
RACE RACE RACE RACE RACE RAC  **Un-name**  ACE
ACE RACE RACE RACE RACE RACE RACE RA  **Feint**
CE RACE RACE RACE RACE RACE RACE RACE  **Vein**
E RACE RACE RACE RACE RACE RACE  **Rain**  REST
RACE RACE RACE RACE RACE R  **Sane**  EST REST R
ACE RACE RACE RACE R  **Name**  ST REST REST RE
CE RACE RACE RA  **Face**  EST REST REST REST RES
E RACE RAC  **Space**  T REST REST REST REST REST
RACE  **Solace**   REST REST REST REST REST REST R
**Grace**  T REST REST REST REST REST REST REST RE
T REST REST REST REST REST REST REST REST RES

## Unique Theory

I have this theory
That if we could study
Skin as minutely
As we do DNA stringers
And the print of our fingers
*a.k.a. fingerprints*
Then we would find difference
That the skin of us each
Is just as unique
As these other things

## Socio-economic Schisms:

**Wealthy Miens**

Wealth is a means
To do things

It doesn't mean
A person is mean
Or prove their miens
It only is a means

A person's things
That have true meaning
Are the internal things
That have learned to sing
In joy and suffering

## Guarantees and Securities

Poverty is no
Guarantee of
Purity or honor

Money is no
Security of
Impunity or health

Lack or abundance
Are no evidence
Of resilience
Only a test
Of your true self

They prove
What's inside of you
Already
Before the test began
They show
If you can stand

# Suspending Schisms:

**Brutality**

Brutality is nothing new
Gruesome
Is stale, moldy bread, too

Pain expression
Through aggression
Ain't
A new thang

It's trite and passe
A waste of space
It's so
Twenty minutes ago

If you want to do a new thing
If you want to be trending
Then create a way
To express your pain
Without hurting yourself
Or anyone else

No-mas-hate
*(that's Spanglish for "No more hate.")*

## Spew Reveals You

It's this – It's that
It's a bloodbath
All this hate and rage
The world's a troll's stage

Can anyone tell me why?
Critics? Trolls? Sycophants?
What drives your eye?
Greed? Envy? Elephants?

An inward turn
Show some concern
To heal the burn
Your sickly souls yearn

I can't help think
When your words stink
It's a missing link
In your DNA chink

That's not quite right
I think your blight
Stems from your sight
Soul's darkest night

Your hate is pain
You fear to name
Instead you stain
Those who are same

Your shame you hide
Evil words behind
Buried alive
No one can find

It's time to end
Foaming madness
It's time to mend
Wounds poisonous
It's time to bend
To truthfulness
It's time to spend
Words on peace

> Come clean – Come true
> The best you can do
> Cease the hate spew
> Release yourself, too

# 4 – SILENT SCREAMS

## *Chapter Four - Introduction*

Silent screams are an outcry of pain and torment for those whose voice has been denied, defiled and reviled. These internal screams are an appeal, a demand for justice The silent screams are seen in the eye of the one suffering.

If a person screams in the middle of a world saturated with incessant, insistent noise, does this person's voice matter? Is their cause heard? Will justice respond?

Even if you think no one's listening, speak. Someone you don't know is listening for a voice like yours to say exactly what you have to say.

Even if your voice doesn't immediately change anything, speak. Someone you don't see is watching for someone like you to say something, to speak out against the noise, to shine a light in the darkness that surrounds us and threatens to engulf us all.

Even if no one is by your side, speak. Someone who is nowhere near you needs to hear your voice and what you have to say because they believe (are deceived) that they are alone and no one knows, understands or cares. But if they hear you speak – *your* words spoken with *your* voice – then they can choose to receive comfort, encouragement and be revived in their own fight.

Your voice matters. It carries. Someone is listening. Someone is waiting. Speak.

## Burned Soul Recovering

The nauseating process to heal:

Scab
    Peel
        Scream
            Feel
                Sleep

Scab
    Peel
        Scream
            Feel
                Sleep

Scab
    Peel
        Scream
            Feel
                Sleep

Scab
    Peel
        Scream
            Feel
                Sleep

Scab
    Peel
        Scream
            Feel
                Sleep

Repeat for as long as I need.

## Empty words

Empty words
No purpose
Littering
Atmosphere

Void of power
Obscurely sour
What they don't devour
They disempower

These empty words
Clutter the ground
People in hordes
Stumble around

Noise pollution
Foolish effusion
Dishing confusion
Absent solution

Hearing sound
To expound
Nonsense found
Noise abounds

It's not enough
To be silent
When this stuff
Is violent

Words of intent
Must stem the vent
Vie to protect
The innocent

Empty words
Are a curse
As if their verse
Could truth disperse

They don't contain
Life in their vein
Death is their rein
Until then in vain

Their purpose to diffuse
The effect of truth
It's nothing new
All the same to you

## Fallen Mentality

Evil is good
Lying is truth
That is the poop
We've bought into

One lone critic
Can ruin it
Lead us to doubt
Blind our words out

Just one wee troll
Snake biting tongue
Slashes at throat
Leaving us numb

Down with evil
Reign of shame
Rebuking hate
Cuz ain't my name

## Psalming

I am afraid that if I speak
Then that gives her access
To my life, my soul

I'm afraid that if I interact
With her, then she'll
Syphon me

I am afraid that she owns
And controls my voice
Still

I'm afraid that all I am is
A reaction to her abuse and
Violence against my sanctity

I'm afraid that I can't be
Myself with her

I'm afraid that I'm still her
Puppet

I'm afraid that her darkness
Blots out Your light

I'm afraid that her definition
Of me will dominate
Take over and control me like before

I'm afraid that her
Lies are truth

When I look at her
I can't see the Light

She is madness and
Won't turn from it

I am afraid that her reality
Will silence me and
Murder the truth I believe

                                      Lift up my eyes
                                      Into the Light
                                      That confounds darkness
                                      Drives fear to flee
                                      Overcomes all infirmity
                                      Including soul-syphoning

                                      Return to the One
                                      Who is Love
                                      Who has won
                                      And reigns above

## Power Diabolical Dynamics

Lucifer
Is an equal opportunity
Employer

                                      And

If you submit to be his partner
He'll use you
To perpetrate murder

                                      Yet

No power
He wields can ever triumph over
God's pure love

## Wooly Mammoth

It's like she's
Gnawing me

She's a little chihuahua
Gnawing on the little toe
Of a wooly mammoth
As if that could do damage

It hurts – her yapping
Biting snapping snarling
And it annoys me

I could crush her
In an instant
If the inclination
Hit

But
That's not who I am

I don't want
To crush or hurt

I just
Want her to shut up
And prance
Her little prissy ass
Someplace else

She yaps and yaps
Senselessly saps
A voice of noise
Draining void

She yammers on
Hammers anon

We're not in the same game or same league
Yet she lunges to leagues to attack me
We're not even in the same species
Yet she hates me specifically

Maybe if I just nudge
Her over a small ledge
Too tall for her
To conquer
Too short for her
To be harmed

Then mosey away
To a quiet place
Live out my days
In a restful pace

              Sigh
              I

## Wreckage

When I look at
The wreckage
I feel defeated

When I see how
She affected me
I feel so much grief

How could she
How cold she

How was it easy for her
To hurt me
How could I mean
So little

I don't want the damage
To become my identity
I don't want the wreckage
To remain on me

How can I
How am I

# 5 – LAMENTS

## *Chapter Five - Introduction*

Laments are expressions of a heavy heart, one weighed down by sorrow and loss. The heart does not find rest or peace until the suffering is given an outward expression – be that expression in sighs, groans, sobs, words, art, lyrics, or any other safe means that bring relief.

Laments release what lingers in the soul, trapped beneath the things that strive to silence a soul. This process of lamenting expunges emotions and gives relief to the voice within that aches to be heard, known and understood.

Laments are the way to honor our internal selves and permit those around us insight into our internal lives. They allow us to grieve. They let us begin to feel peace again. They make room for new life and new experiences. They are the process by which we move from the place of less and loss to the place of peace, growth, breakthrough and gain – on this journey of life.

# A Processing Passage

The anointing of grief
Came over me
I wrote so much poetry
That my eyes did bleed
I swiped left
Yet still bereft

                        Oh my gosh!
                        Make it stop!

My heart poured
As if gored
I couldn't cease
The endless release
Poetry and prose
Dripped like my nose

                        Put the pen down
                        Before I drown!

I blew and blue
And wrote some, too
The perpetual rain
Delivered me sane
Eventually
Across the sea…

                        And…finally
                        I can *not*
                                    think

## Brother's Lament

A seared soul
A blackhole
Cannot know
What is whole

Seared clear through.
Whoever knew!
Human too?
Ever was new?

Innocence
Stolen hence
Too young when
Rooster hens

Would that I
Could have…I
Can't think…I

                         Feel so powerless
                         Against the madness
                         Of their vile violence

I can't save
I am brave
But all they
Did was hate

I miss him
Innocent
Before his
Dark descent

He was sweet
Purity
Smiling free

Until…the enemy…

Defiled his
Innocence
With madness
Violence

                                      This one
                                      Twisted tortured
                                      Into oblivion

I see no
Heart or soul
In him, though
I still hope

I have to
Hope that You
Can yet do
Something new

Dry bones can
Breathe again

                                      For You can
                                      Sovereign

I hope for the boy
My brother once was
Though I see no remnant
No life in his extant
I pray yet because
I hope for the boy
That once was

## Lament for a Sister

Her unwillingness to repent
Is the vein of my lament

She doesn't want forgiveness
She wants my submissiveness

If she admits who I am
Then she knows I can't

The heart is the matter she hides
Behind layers of half-truths & lies

She refuses to leave her prison cell
Perhaps because she knows it too well

She perceives the pain
It costs her to remain
As smaller than the shame
Of forgiveness in Your name

My heart aches
To restore again
The loss quakes
Is my hope in vain?

## Proverbs of Prisoners (*or* Proverbial Prisoners)

A prison break
is not their way.

The door is open,
yet they close it.

They eschew liberty
to choose slavery.

They prefer to lie
where, when truth dies.

Hostages held
By themselves.

No one to blame.
They chose this shame.

The prisoner's dilemma:
victor or victim?

## They're – Their – There

I'm here
They're there

I left
Their there

They won't leave there
Because in their
Minds I'm not, they're

Leaving their
Wicked there
Severed they're
From my there

**Truth Truce**

She spoke
Her truth

I fell
Flat ground
On down

I stared
She glared
teeth bared
Not scared

Faced off
She sought
my naught
I thought
her taught

Mask gone
I saw
her maw
She rejected
I accepted
Then freedom

Grief came
Washed drain
Down pain
Blood vein
Cleaned name

Let go
my hold
No gold
to show

Sad lose
Her choose
to use

Loose I
Let sigh

My truth

## Wising Up

Arguing with the senseless
Is like jumping into quicksand
And believing that all your struggling
And thrashing about
Will get you free
But rather your arguments
With senselessness
Simply drag you faster and deeper
Down into the suffocating pit

Arguing with the senseless
Destroys you
And changes them not

They remain
Insane
Demanding
You join in

# 6 – BALM

## Chapter Six – Introduction

Balm is the poetry of letting go of unforgiveness and allowing ourselves to forgive our offenders and ourselves. This is the poetry of processing a release that sets us free.

Unforgiveness is a choice. It is a mechanism to keep pain in place. Its design is to punish and torment. Except such a device is far more, and often only, vindictive to the one who withholds forgiveness. Our offenders and attackers rarely, if ever, suffer because we refuse to forgive them. When we hold onto pain, bitterness and resentment, then we are the ones who suffer agony.

Forgiveness does NOT erase the offence nor ignore the harm done by the offender. Forgiveness does NOT mean that no legal action should be taken.

Forgiveness is about accepting what happened, acknowledging and processing the harm done, and releasing the offender's debt to God. Forgiveness is letting go of bitterness and resentment. Forgiveness is trusting the earthly justice system to do its part. More than this, forgiveness is trusting God's justice to be sufficient. Forgiveness is for the one who was harmed, to release the soul from the poison of resentment and the addiction to retaliation.

Forgiveness is about taking the offender's power away – their power to hold a person down, perpetually torment the person with the mere memory of the offense and steal the person's life away through obsession with revenge which leaves no room in a person's life for peace, joy or healthy living.

Forgiveness is about taking back a person's power through accepting what happened, accepting feelings related to the offense, accepting what was stolen in the offense, and accepting the Lord's help to heal and restore every part of a person that was affected by the attack. God has a plan to redeem everything. Vengeance belongs to Him alone who is Perfect and the only One able to orchestrate flawless justice and the ultimate recompense.

Forgiveness is also about accepting that we have all offended someone, are deserving of punishment for our offenses and yet God shows us mercy.

Forgiveness is, more often than not, about forgiving ourselves. It is about ceasing the incessant self-blame for someone else's rotten choices to harm us. We are not the reason that they chose to harm. Forgiveness is about accepting that we do not have control over others. We only have control over ourselves and our choices. That is where our strength lies – in acceptance, in forgiveness, in moving through the process and in owning those responsibilities that are only under our control.

## A day stained in blood

A day stained in blood
A day in infamy

Being with them
For their rancid conduct
Takes up
Too much energy

I no longer fear
Their evil deeds
No longer cling to me

I turn to give
Myself to grieve

I simply am to be
Cut free from the chains
Of my enemy

It seems
I've somehow come to agree
That their evil deeds
Are not me

I feel separate
I feel sad for their choices
I grieve what waits for them

I release myself
From their unhealth

I sit with this
Separateness
Newly found
I allow it to marinate

Into my bones

I am not
What they do
Their shame
Cannot touch me
I am
Not them

## Accepting Rejection

You said
       Friend
You did
       Enemy

I heard what you said
I saw what you did

In my desperation
I ignored your rejection

I knew
The truth
About you

But I lied
To myself
Deceived
So I could pretend
You met my need

I did not heed
Any of your deeds

I did not believe
When you told me
You were my enemy

I rejected
Your rejection
And in so doing
Rejected my own dignity

Forgive me
For pretending

You were friendly
And liked me

I shudder sorrowfully
I did not honor your deeds

I accept your rejection of me
I accept you will not friend me
I accept you are my enemy
I accept the end of you and me

I accept you
I accept me
        without you

## Blanking Out…and In…Again

Sometimes
        the page is blank
        because I feel blank
        because I have nothing to say
        because the words can't escape
        from the dark place

Sometimes
        all I have is
        the nothingness
        emptiness
        abyss

Sometimes
        it's all I can do to breathe
        and just be
        allow myself to grieve

Sometimes
        my only thought
        is to accept the loss

Sometimes
        I am enough

**Creative Grace**

The stumble, the smudge
Do not begrudge
The unexpected process
Emerging from the mess

A wonderful product
You never intended to construct

There are no mistakes
There is only more paint

## Deep Dive Derive

Submerged beneath
Surface not so deep
Flashlight in hand
Floating over sand

I shined the light
In a cave at night
Sharks inert
Now burst forth

Fear swam over my mind
As I sputtered blind
Sharks turned benign
At least that night

Other sharks beneath
Surface of murky seas
Have been less likely
To *not* bite me

Lessons learned in a dive
May yet keep me alive
And from entering a dive
Which few survive

Lessons to guide
Toward abide
Find free from strife
Peace, joy, good – Life

## Fear of the Lord

I'm too afraid
Not to tell Him
What's in my heart

If I hold it in
It keeps us apart
Of THAT, I am afraid

There is no part
However far strayed
Can't return to Him

In only Him
Is my heart
Unafraid

**Floating**

Floating
Is about letting go

The water
Isn't the problem

Quieting and trusting
While in the water
Is the test

The rebellion
Of self-reliance

The defiance
Of connection

Let go to become bold
In ways not known
On waves yet told,
                    "Peace!  Be still."

## Humanity Restored

When we support a person healing their soul
Our humanity is restored
And from the healthy overflow
We're all better equipped to nurture our world

## Never Was Until

I'm not enough
>Unable I was
>To earn Your love

Accepting of
>I never was
>Without Your love

I'm not the loss
>I thought I was
>Until Your love

## Not in So Many Steps

Being lifted out
Of the pit
Is a good thing
But not
The last thing

I'm still me
A change of location
Doesn't make me whole

I'm recovering
Walking out
My transforming soul
With awe and wonder

As I gaze on the Face
Of the One
Who surrendered
All to take my place
In that rancid pit
Even for a moment

Even when
I walk alone
I know my soul
Is at Home

# Responses

I feel a wash of relief
To consider *not* responding

The mere thought
Of a response
Feels like holding up
My arms if to stop
A giant tidal wave
Of her violent hate

When I put my arms down
And turn away and around
The wave vanishes
To a ripple of ashes
Rolling out to oblivion
In a powerful peace of ocean
That has no space or patience
For any vent of violence

Love's ocean is infinite
*Her* vent is transient

## Six to One to Seven

They have no part with me
Though they are known to me

The connection ends
With their violence

They who once knew
Now reject truth

I am sad
They chose bad

Goodbye
Their lie

Done
Sun

Inhale
Exhale

I can breathe
With their leave

Freedom in free
From villainy

At last I can rest
Free from their madness

Their curses did nothing
An end to suffering

I moved through tears to laughter
I shall gain more ever-after

### Today

Today is enough
To just let You touch
These scabby places
The poisoned traces
That need violent relief
From holding in grief

## Unforgiveness – Unto the Breach

I ached to be absolved
But she refused

I longed to bare my soul
And repent for each and all

But she would not
Acknowledge even the thought

She spurned my plea
I fell in infamy

I begged for death's relief
You came to me

                                      The only true rescue
                                      Is Your pure love above

                                      I accepted Your pardon
                                      Gave myself my own
                                      And let hope for hers go
                                      And her, too, I let go


Unforgiveness_____
                                                                           Is a chasm
Breached only by_____
                                                                           Acceptance

# 7 – BREAKING GROUND

## Chapter Seven - Introduction

Breaking ground is about hope. It is about seeds unseen growing underneath the cover of a nutrient rich soil. Hope is found in waiting for the good that is yet to be revealed. It is a delicious expectation and an excited perseverance. It is trust in the promises of a future and a life that is filled with wonder, adventure, beauty and excellence.

Hope is a kindled fire in the heart of the one who hopes. This fire burns through doubt, despair, delay and anything else thrown in its way. It does not give up nor does it give in. Its anchor is in the future authenticity unseen yet *not* unknown in the heart of the hoper.

Hope is the rallying battle-cry before the battle begins, knowing and trusting that the battle is already settled and won. It is faithful defiance in the face of accusations of madness and foolishness. It is impenetrably resolute in the crux of abandonment and the desertion of less faithful companions. Hope is the undeterred belief in the forthcoming victory.

Hope is an unshakable faith in a reality yet to be realized and a trust in a life to come that is above and beyond this one. Hope is a thing already decided – inside a person's heart.

## Confidence

If I thought to pray for it
Then I'm probably made for it

## Diminishing Darkness

You and I were made
To dance on the waves
Even when storms rage

To climb mountains high
To sparkle and shine
Even when dark is the night

We are never diminished
By the circumstances
That surround us

## Empty Me Full

Empty me out
Here and now
Remove every last semblance
Every last raging menace
Of longing for human affection

Rob me right and true
Of what I never knew
Cast me headlong into the torrent
Suffering and sorrow spent
Now have I Your attention?

Knock on all of the doors
I am only ever Yours
I have lost all taste for life
I am surrendered; no strife
All I have is devotion

Losing self
Felt like hell
But shallow was that loss
Changing to gold from dross
Faithful and true emotion

I have won
All the love
My barren heart's thirst
Delights in forever and first
The greatest exultation

Your heart I trust
Be true and just
Throughout eternity
We share in all things
You are my highest exaltation

## I Am Still

I am still me
Even when I have

> No family
> No money
> No purpose to be
> No intentionality
> No home
> Nowhere to roam
> Nothing I own
> No one
> Nothing to do
> No seeming use
> No one to love, too
> No one but You

With You
     I am still

## Out of the Chasm

Hope
Awakened
Within
The chasm

Beckoned
    By the light
    Beyond comprehension

Quickened
    By the love
    Of the Ascended One

Reckoned
    Worthy of
    Sacrificial love

*and*

Named
    By the heart
    Of radiant affection

### Pockets of Silence

I'm no longer living in pockets
Of silence carved out of
Niches in the violence

I'm living and breathing in
Increasing freedom taken back
From the thief whose time is slack

## Questioning Statements

Disengaging
Who these shackles enring

Loosing
What grip fear had on me

Forgetting
Where ignominy

Remembering
How far You've brought me

Questioning
When's the next thing

## Securing Room for Trust

You are on the move
Even if I do naught
Even when I am at rest
In Your presence

My trust
Is Your room
To be You

## Steps of Faith

Each step on the waves
Is an act of faith

Every moment on the water
Reminds me that you are my Father

I could not stand here
If I looked to fear

If I turned away from Your face
I would drown in the sound
Of the voice denying my choice
To stand in faith on Your name
More solid ground could not be found
To hold my poise against the noise

Your love alone
Is my hope

# 8 – EQUITABLE RESTITUTION

## *Chapter Eight - Introduction*

The devil, that thieving marauder, must repay sevenfold what he stole (Proverbs 6:31). This chapter is the poetry of recompense, restitution and a full equitable distribution for what has been taken from us by our mutual enemy, the devil.

This poetry is the fruit of trusting in the Lord's plan for restoration and redemption. It is the blessing received through giving the Lord room to be Himself and do what only He can do.

This is the gift of sleeping in the boat on a storm-tossed sea even while the boat is taking on water. This is enjoying a sumptuous feast even while your enemies are nearby, watching in envy and writhing in wrath. This is knowing peace at all times no matter what is going on around you. This is rest in seasons of distress, enmity and ignominy. This is living above the fray and from a place of victory. This is a seat of confidence firmly established on the bedrock of faith.

## Definitions of Value

You are not defined
>by what you do
>or what other
>people think of you

Your value
>is not up to you
>you're worthy
>because God loves you

## Fast Finite

A sacrifice
of worldly delights

fasting is
hungering for You
to break on through
the dark of night

to kindle light
my soul inside
breathes Kingdom air
eyes blazing fair

such food extant
of my stomach
feeds my loves heart
which is was start

begin end infinite
behind time is light
I know not without
all true in His house

a fast of sight
on this finite
ends other side
eternal life

## Mercy and the Sea

Mercy
Is the currency
That sets me free

                    The current
                    That carries me
                    To sea

                    The water
                    That washes me
                    Clean

Mercy
Gives me
Something to bring

                    A song
                    When I have nothing
                    But me

                    A light
                    Shining brightly
                    Within me

Mercy
Is the story
of how He won me

                    The flood
                    Of His love
                    That released me

                    The waves
                    Of His praise
                    That fill my days

## Normally Speaking

There is nothing
Normal under the sun
All that matters is His blood
Truth is enough is enough
The only victory is Love

## Not in a Moment

I walk about freely
In peace and harmony
As if I never knew
Any kind of misuse

What you see in me now
Took years to plant and plow
Leaving was the first step
In battles that tested
Every part of me
Requiring that I leave
Everything I'd known
To walk through fire alone

Year after year
Tears upon tears
Never knowing the end
A constant descent

Fleeting wisps of hope
Promises of a love unknown

Victory doesn't come in a moment
It comes in perseverance
That knows no end
Simply because it won't give in

Victory doesn't come in a two-hour movie
It comes in a wilderness of undoing
It doesn't come without scars of betrayal
Nor without marks of pain and sorrow

Wisdom that doesn't come from a limp
Is not the wisdom of experience

The victory you see in me
Comes from years of fighting
The invitation to surrender
To the One who is tender

The character and resilience
You see in my countenance
Was hard fought
And hard won

It did not come on day one
But over time sunk into my bones
Purifying my inner soul

It became what I know
The reality I walk in
The victory I am in Him

**Resting Repentance**

I don't know
What I know
But
My spirit knows
And
It pours forth
Tears of sorrow
Peace and joy
Songs of praise
To the One who raised
My life out of the fray
And led my feet
From the grave
Into a place
Of quiet and trust
Of repent and rest

## That I Am

I want to sing
To do that thing
I was made to bring

I want to live
In that I give
Love is no sieve

I want to roar
All in heart stored
My voice is Yours, Lord

I want the sound
To shake the ground
Prison doors open found

I want this pain
To not be in vain
Washed in Your name

This road we walk
Cannot be all talk
From that I balk

Our journey through
Must end in You
Tears to joy, true

I will take Your hand
Because I know You can
Restore all that I am

## The Beloved

I am not defined
By the violence
I survived

I am defined by
Jesus Christ
Who gave me life

I am His victory
My life story
Tells of His glory

I am
    the
    Beloved

## The Shore

I can't go back to the shore
It doesn't seem real to me anymore

I must go
        where angels dare not tred
Or I will
        succumb this living death

I must be
        wherever You lead me
I am not
        without Your heartbeat

# 9 – FANNING THE FLAME

*Chapter Nine – Introduction*

There is an influx of energy and motivation in the heart of a person who has overcome a setback, a season of lack or some heinous attack. The process of overcoming, of conquering, of enduring awakens a soul to purpose. It opens a person's eyes to what fire burns inside of them.

This is the poetry of overcoming trials and persevering through temptation so that a person is refined, entrusted and empowered in the process. This is the poetry of fanning the flame of desire to make an impact, to lead a life of meaning. This is the poetry of embarking on a mission that a person was designed from the start to live and breathe and be.

## Breakable Power

You're not as powerful_____
                                   as you feel you are

You're not as breakable_____
                    _____as you fear you are

You're not as alone
                _____as you think you are

## Breaking Binds

I break agreement
With achievement

I silence
The insanity
Of never-ending
People-pleasing

i wrestle with all of
my insecurity
grappling on the ground
a knock-down-drag-out
kicking and screaming bout

wrenching to be released
from this violent beast
that stalks and torments me
daily ceaselessly

I must release my mind
From its unholy bind

With words as sharp
As double-edged swords
I fight through the lies
Of the one I despise

With holy revelation
I silence the deviant one
And break loose
The bonds of his abuse

With my eyes clean
And my heart set free
I look around me

For others in need

I share freely
With all who need
Loves refreshing
Balm of healing

With every act of mercy
I slice through the lies
Of the enemy's disguise
I reveal God's glory

## Courage Found Waves

No courage is found
Staying on the ground

---

The boat is safe
               Dancing on waves
               Is a nice change
Rowing away

---

The boat moves not
Raging winds fought
               Walking in thought
               As Him I sought

---

                              My courage is bound
                              To His voice song sound

## Elevation

When a child of God
    Seeks to please
        A man-made system
    Works to measure up
        To a worldly construct
That child is then operating
    Under a lower view
        A lesser dominion

Wherever a child of God stands
The Kingdom of God is at hand

Sons and daughters
Of the King of Heaven
Elevate
Whatever place
They invade
With the Light of Heaven
Within their hearts

## Embodiment

I stand in the gap
that is essential
to protect your back

Mainly, your effect,
though providential,
without me is less

You cannot achieve
our full potential
until you receive

The side I am on
at times torrential
is the same you're on

Align to yourself
the One essential
aligned to myself

Amen
      my friend

# Grasshoppers

*Prosperity of soul is this:*
> That the Lord's righteousness
> Is infused so
> Deep in my soul
> Even the Anakites
> Are as grasshoppers in my sight

## Hate with Love

To fight hate with love
Is what a martyr does

They sacrifice their life
To set others free from strife

Their death is gain
For those who remain

## Identity Stirring

Brave enough
              to endure and to survive


Strong enough
              to fight and recover all


Bright enough
              to light the way for others

## Obedient Love

Obedience – eyes wide open
Is the expression of love
In faithfulness

                                      Obedience – lids shut tight
                                      Is the violent demand
                                      Of dull tyrants

                                      Gang leaders demand it
                                      Drug lords command it
                                      Sex slaves suffer in it

                                      All that is wicked
                                      Writhes under this law
                                      Distorted rule

                                      They hate the Lord
                                      Who gave this word
                                      A pure meaning

Love must find expression
Faith must be evident
In freedom obedient

Love is a weapon
The enemy's response
Is fear and flight
From obedience right

Words are not enough
For the proof of love

To wrestle with the enemy
Is to love humanity
Which is far from lovely
And gives back nothing

The war is here
Whom do you fear?

*Or rather:*
                Who has your willing
                And true obedience?

## Standardizing

High standards

>Are not filled
>In the valley lows

>>Nor found
>>In the depraved folk

>Are unearthed
>In the refiner's fire

>>And purified
>>On lone mountain heights

If excellence were universal
Then these would be

Common standards

## Treading the Waves

My Lord has led
My life to tred
Upon the waves

What is land to me?
Just another place
The Lords sets my feet

These stormy waves
For me were made

It's not that I was made
To walk upon the waves

But that the wind & waves
For my delight were made
To satisfy my soul

He allowed the storm to rain
So that I would know
He is Sovereign

The depths of grief & pain
Cannot overcome His name

But in their searing flames
I am set free again

## Unsettling Discoveries

I feel a contentment
That has awakened
A deeper hunger

An appetite satisfied
Has opened my senses
To unknown discontent

The fullness is only temporary
Meant just to carry me
Through a new famine

My thirst is slaked
To stave off the coming drought
Until return the thunderclouds

This bounty is only
Meant to kindle
A fiercer fire

The longing expanded
The need further exposed
The ache increasingly understood

I am less than I saw
And more than I knew
Empty without You

All I am is in You
All I have needs You
All is nothing, except You

## Voicing Influence

Death cannot silence
The voice of a human life

My impact and influence
Do not end with my last breath

## Want for Naught

The world waits
For me to say
That my faith
Is found in safe
Free from strain

That something less
Than the nothingness
Burning insignificance
Crucifying selfishness
Of forging fire tests

The world waits
For me to say
That my way
Led me from pain
And the horrid fray

All of them want
To believe un-daunt
In a life walk
That has no fraught
Wins without fought

It's not my story
To deny Your glory
This life's been gory
But Your victory
Is ALL of my story

## You Are

You are who you are
You do what you do
                This time's you

No one else
Nothing less
            Defines you

## Waves

I was created brave
Unafraid and unashamed

I will *not* yield to fear
It has no place here

I made the choice a while ago
There's no other option for my soul

The waves may come
But I remain in Love

No matter what it costs me
I am in this for His Love for me

# 10 - HERBS

## Chapter Ten - Introduction

Herbs are the seasoning of wisdom gained through learning from real and raw experience and growing character under the gentle microscope of self-examination.

It is a waste of this life to refuse to gain or benefit from what we experience. Consider an athlete. They engage in a competition. Then afterwards, they examine their performance – acknowledging their successful actions and paying particular attention to their unsuccessful or thwarted actions. They spend additional time and effort analyzing ways to improve their performance, increase their probability of success and protect their areas of weakness and vulnerability. This is wisdom.

Let us live our lives in the same way as an athlete by examining our actions, our motives, our experiences and considering where we can improve. Deem mistakes, weaknesses, failures and exposed vulnerabilities as information to be used to refine the character, heart, choices, words and actions. *This* is what it means to be growing wisdom in the garden of our hearts.

I chose thirty-seven poems for this chapter because David had thirty-seven mighty men fighting with him (see 2 Samuel 23:8-39) while he traversed his season in the wilderness of persecution and rejection. Wisdom comes from experience, from being battle-tested and from the sparks that fly in a community that is willing to navigate conflict and does not fear confrontation.

## *One*
I join my prayer
With all the saints there

## _Two_
Begin each day
From a place of rest
This is the Kingdom
Recipe for success

### *Three*
Let me rest in Your embrace
And find solace in Your holy gaze

### _Four_
Am I?
> *I choose you.*

Am I?
> *I am with you.*

Am I?
> *I delight in you.*

Am I?
> *I have good plans for you.*

Am I?
> *I loved you before time began.*

Am I?
> *I give my life to save you.*

Am I?
> *I am yours.*

### *Five*
The truth without love
Is *not* from the Kingdom above

It is the pursuit of death
Destruction is its breath

Being right
Is its might

Being good
misunderstood

It has no mind
To be kind

### *Six*
Flattery is no equivalent
To a complement

There are no strings
With sincerity

If it has strings
It's the other thing

### *Seven*
How could I stand on the heights
Unless I first knelt in the depths?

### *Eight*
The safest space
in any storm
is the pure light
of fiery eyes
piercing and warm
that grace God's face

### *Nine*
Unkindness is nothing to me now
That I am a vessel – hollowed out

## *Ten*
Your love is my vindication
Your blood is my vengeance
Our relationship is my freedom
My victory is Your truth
My value is Who You Are
Surrendered to freedom

## *Eleven*
You're already a broken mess.
All you have to do is say, "Yes!"

## *Twelve*
People who
> pursue change
> do change

### _Thirteen_
With words or with swords
Shall I go to war, my Lord?

### *Fourteen*
To receive offense
Is too frivolous
Of an expense
To spend against us

### *Fifteen*
Pretension provokes dissension
As bitterness churns up bile

### *Sixteen*
Prayer is more than enough
In all seasons and all times
To release the Kingdom of Heaven
Over people's lives

### *Seventeen*
You can't gain respect
By dishing disrespect

Ditch disrespect
Multiply respect

### _Eighteen_
I don't want your pity
It steals my dignity

I need your compassion
It lets me be human
And shows me you are, too
It gives us a chance to be seen through

### _Nineteen_
Tribulation
Is not only preparation
But also a spirit's edification
On how to bring its flesh into submission
Unto a warrior's transformation

It is an invitation
To grant permission
To God's redemption
Over every situation
You enter in
For His glorification

### *Twenty*
I am too poor and humble to afford
Knee-jerk reacting to an injurious word

Such assaults cannot touch my soul
While I seek Your mysteries to know

### _Twenty-one_
When it's the right time
The Lord will bring it to mind

## *Twenty-two*
Suppressing
          is not the same as
                        Processing

### _Twenty-three_
Unless I first knew
The strength of You
To lead me through
And enable me to stand there
Even in the depths of despair

How could I ever breathe mountain air?

### *Twenty-four*
Letting go of the rest
To know alone Your rest

### *Twenty-five*
The road of hate
Paved with dominate

Cobbled with
Stones quarried from
Caverns of *fear of love*

Leading nowhere
But despair

## *Twenty-six*
Had I never surrendered my self-reliance
How could I ever delight in the dance?

### *Twenty-seven*
The fury and malice of abuse
Has no life nor light of truth

### *Twenty-eight*
everything you need
is found
in worshipping Me
unbound
from self-sufficiency
around
your insecurity

your identity
is sound
on ground
that is made of Me

### _Twenty-nine_
The change in me
That I pursue
Is the victory
I win for us, too

### *Thirty*
There is no shame
In following Your leading

*There* is Your grace
And knowing more in mystery

### *Thirty-one*
Wherever I see impassibility
You are infinite creativity

### *Thirty-two*
To embrace humility
Is to despise humiliation

To become humble
Is to be exalted over shame

### *Thirty-three*
Wherever I see a roadblock
You see a mindset to unblock

## *Thirty-four*
Favoritism is a trade for favors
Whereas favor shows no favoritism

***Thirty-five***
Repentance stirs up relentance
In one prone to compassion

***Thirty-six***
My work today
Is to love and play

### *Thirty-seven*

If you look to me
For answers and remedies
I only got one thing to say
*Jesus*
His life death resurrection is
The truth you seek and the way

# EPILOGUE

## Pandemic Comment

Some of you might be wondering
How this author could mention nothing
About the pandemic COVID-19
Others of you might find it a relief

I do grieve this pandemic
It took a toll with much affect
Our lives forever altered
As our world faltered
Under the menace
Of an unseen virus
With the vaccine release
We begin to move toward peace
Even so
The future holds
What? – We don't know
All too well now – We know

Along the way
I've got to say
*That* pandemic
Wasn't as systemic
As the ones that remain
And continue to stain
Every aspect of humanity
With their heinous insanity

Let's examine and discuss
Some of these pandemics hideous:

Sexual abuse
              that soul-sucking noose

Human trafficking
                      that inhumane desecrating
Abuse of any other form
                      that degrading storm

Sexism – Age-ism – Socio-economic-ism – Racism
Any and every other dehumanizing schism
That pursues killing and destroying
The sanctity of any human being

The greatest pandemic we face
Is anything that separates
Us from wisdom, compassion
Generous living and connection

Anything that promotes
Jealousy and selfishness
Is the thing that demotes
Humanity and loving kindness

We cannot win
When our own conduct
Is the problem
That gets us stuck

Let's do something to stop the madness –
Partner with the cause that stirs up your passion

Unite with the people who fight
For every person to have life
Honorable and dignified
Saved and sanctified

Honoring free will
To live the life they will

**About the Author:**

Rebecca Anne Perry is a poet, painter and wandering Texan who is, for now, quietly planted in the bustling metropolis of Los Angeles. She counts her trials, tests, tragedies and triumphs as events that impart wisdom and inform her relationships. When she's not writing, she enjoys baking, reading and lounging in a hammock.

*A verse which inspires
this writer's voice:*

*Psalm 107:2*

## Other books by Rebecca Anne Perry available on Amazon.com:

❖ Onions – peeling back the layers; poetry in the process of recovering from trauma

❖ Jugular – words of warfare

Leave a review on Amazon.com to share your thoughts, impressions & recommendations for each book that you read. Your voice matters!

www.ingramcontent.com/pod-product-compliance
Lightning Source LLC
Chambersburg PA
CBHW022104090426
42743CB00008B/710